鳥　山　明

Grrr. The one thing I am truly terrified of happened again. The cavity that I ignored, because I hate going to the dentist, started to get painful. It was the day of my deadline, but the pain was so bad I couldn't even sleep. I couldn't bear it any longer, so I ran to the dentist, only to find out I was too late: the tooth had to be pulled. So then I had to work on my manga while bearing the pain of my just-extracted tooth. It was pretty much my fault, but it was still the worst, most awful day I've ever had.

—*Akira Toriyama, 1990*

Artist/writer Akira Toriyama burst onto the manga scene in 1980 with the wildly popular **Dr. Slump**, a science fiction comedy about the adventures of a mad scientist and his android "daughter." In 1984 he created his hit series **Dragon Ball**, which ran until 1995 in Shueisha's best-selling magazine **Weekly Shonen Jump**, and was translated into foreign languages around the world. Since **Dragon Ball**, he has worked on a variety of short series, including **Cowa!**, **Kajika**, **SandLand**, and **Neko Majin**, as well as a children's book, **Toccio the Angel**. He is also known for his design work on video games, particularly the **Dragon Warrior** RPG series. He lives with his family in Japan.

DRAGON BALL Z VOL. 5
The SHONEN JUMP Manga Edition

This manga is number 21 in a series of 42.

STORY AND ART BY
AKIRA TORIYAMA

English Adaptation/Gerard Jones
Translation/Lillian Olsen
Touch-Up Art & Lettering/Wayne Truman
Cover Design/Izumi Evers & Dan Ziegler
Graphics & Design/Sean Lee
Original Editors/Trish Ledoux & Jason Thompson
Graphic Novel Editor/Jason Thompson

Managing Editor/Frances E. Wall
Editorial Director/Elizabeth Kawasaki
Editor in Chief, Books/Alvin Lu
Editor in Chief, Magazines/Marc Weidenbaum
Sr. Director of Acquisitions/Rika Inouye
Sr. VP of Marketing/Liza Coppola
Exec. VP of Sales & Marketing/John Easum
Publisher/Hyoe Narita

In the original Japanese edition, DRAGON BALL and DRAGON BALL Z are known collectively as the 42-volume series DRAGON BALL. The English DRAGON BALL Z was originally volumes 17-42 of the Japanese DRAGON BALL.

Published by VIZ Media, LLC
P.O. Box 77010 • San Francisco, CA 94107

SHONEN JUMP Manga Edition
10 9 8 7 6 5 4 3
First printing, March 2003
Third printing, January 2007

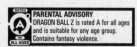

PARENTAL ADVISORY
DRAGON BALL Z is rated A for all ages and is suitable for any age group. Contains fantasy violence.

THE WORLD'S MOST POPULAR MANGA

www.viz.com

www.shonenjump.com

DRAGON BALL Z

Vol. 5

DB: 21 of 42

STORY AND ART BY
AKIRA TORIYAMA

THE MAIN CHARACTERS

Bulma
Goku's oldest friend, Bulma is a scientific genius. She met Goku while on a quest for the seven magical Dragon Balls which, when gathered together, can grant any wish.

Son Goku
The greatest martial artist on Earth, he owes his strength to the training of Kame-Sen'nin and Kaiô-sama, and the fact that he's one of the alien Saiyans. Has he finally hit his limit?

Kaiô-sama
Also known as the "Lord of Worlds", he is one of the deities of the Dragon Ball universe. He lives in the Other World at the end of the Serpent Road.

Kuririn
Goku's former martial arts schoolmate.

Son Gohan
Goku's four-year-old son, a half-human, half-Saiyan with hidden reserves of strength. He was trained by Goku's former enemy Piccolo.

Vegeta

Yajirobe

Yajirobe
A rough-talking, solitary swordsman, never seen without his *katana* sword and *yukata* robes. Yajirobe is one of Goku's old friends, but he's not exactly heroic.

Vegeta
The prince of Planet Vegeta, homeworld of the Saiyans. He claims to be the greatest fighter in the universe. He originally came to Earth to find the Dragon Balls and wish for immortality, but he was defeated… for now…

Kame-Sen'nin

Kame-Sen'nin
Kame-Sen'nin, also known as the "Turtle Hermit" or *Muten-Rôshi* (the "Invincible Old Master"), helped train Goku and Kuririn in the martial arts.

Many years ago, a warlike alien race called the Saiyans sent their young in spaceships to distant worlds, in order to colonize the worlds and kill the inhabitants. One of these young was the baby Son Goku, who overcame his evil heritage and became Earth's greatest hero. Years later, the surviving Saiyans—Vegeta, Nappa, and Goku's brother Raditz—returned to Earth to carry out their original mission of destruction and steal Earth's greatest treasure, the Dragon Balls. Nappa and Raditz, and Goku's friends Yamcha, Tenshinhan, Chaozu and Piccolo died in the assault. After a grueling battle, during which he used the secret techniques taught to him by Kaiô-sama, Goku defeated Vegeta…but now all the survivors lie alongside one another in the rubble, as Vegeta summons his ship to retreat into space…

DRAGON BALL Z 5

CONTENTS

IT'S THE CONTENTS!

DRAGON BALL

DBZ : 47
Goku's Request

LEFT. GOT IT.

A LITTLE MORE... TO THE LEFT...

WHICH WAY?

THAT LIGHT! BENEATH THAT LIGHT!

I TOLD YOU WE SHOULD'VE LEFT HER HOME...

ARE YOU SURE?! ARE YOU *SURE* GOHAN'S ALIVE?!!

I SAID "PROBABLY" !!!

BUT I CAN BARELY FEEL THEIR "CHI"... WHAT'S HAPPENED...?

THERE ARE FOUR OF THEM THERE... OR FIVE...

"PROBABLY" ISN'T GOOD ENOUGH!!!

WHAT ELSE CAN I SAY...?!

BUT THE SAIYAN MUST BE BADLY HURT AS WELL...

GASP

GASP

I...CANNOT SAY... I DID NOT SEE...

VNN--N

Vee--e

AT...
LAST...

SHH
!!!!H

WH...
WHAT...
?

N...
NNN...
UH...!!

•••••

HIS...
SHIP...
!

MUH...
MUST
BE...

HUHH

HUHH

SHK...

SHK...

SO...
CL...
CLOSE...

C...
CURSE
IT ALL...

LET
HIM...
GET
AWAY...
!!

WON'T...

GOTTA... FINISH IT.......

WE'VE COME... THIS FAR...

HUF

HUF

HUF

HUF

I SUPPOSE I SHOULDN'T PLAY FAVORITES, BUT THAT SAIYAN HAS BEEN SO MUCH TROUBLE, ALL OVER THE GALAXY....YES, THIS IS BEST.....

OH, MY....THAT WAS CLOSE... YES, YES, CLOSE INDEED....

12

...IT'S ONLY TOO BAD THAT THIS WON'T DESTROY THE ROOTS OF EVIL...NO, NO, NOT AT ALL...

N...
NNH...

...NOT THE ROOTS........

HFF

HFF

HFF

I CAN'T *MOVE*......!!

N... NO......!!!

!!
!!

DIE!!!!!!!!

THIS... IS FOR EVERYONE... YOU KILLED...!!

HUH?!!!

KURIRIN, *STOP*!!!!

14

GOKU?!

G...

KURIRIN... I HAVE JUST ONE REQUEST...

I'M TOO HURT....TO USE MY VOICE.....

PLEASE... LET THE SAIYAN GO....

W-WAS THAT... YOU, GOKU...?

TALKIN' IN MY HEAD....?

YEAH... PROBABLY...

IF WE LET HIM GO NOW, HE'LL REGAIN HIS STRENGTH AND COME BACK AGAIN!!

HE TRIED TO KILL EVERYBODY IN THE WHOLE WORLD!

A-ARE YOU INSANE?! HE KILLED OUR FRIENDS, HE TRIED TO KILL US...

HE'S NOT LIKE THAT!! HE DOESN'T HAVE A LEAF TO TURN OVER! HE DOESN'T HAVE A SPECK OF DECENCY IN HIM! HE'S A KILLING MACHINE! HE'S A--

ARE YOU THINKING HE'S GONNA SEE THE LIGHT, LIKE PICCOLO? THAT HE'S GONNA TURN OVER A NEW LEAF? WELL, FORGET ABOUT IT!

WHAT A WASTE...

I KNOW... AND I KNOW HOW DANGEROUS, HE IS...

WHAT A ... "WASTE" ?!

BUT... I DON'T KNOW HOW TO SAY IT...WHEN I SAW HIM ABOUT TO DIE... I THOUGHT...

16

BUT VEGETA WAS... SO FAR ABOVE ME...! I WAS SHOCKED... SCARED...

I TRAINED UNDER KAIŌ, THE LORD OF WORLDS... I THOUGHT I'D HIT THE PEAK OF POWER...

DMP...

...RRR...

BUT... SOMEWHERE INSIDE...I WAS HAPPY. I WAS... THRILLED... TO BE FIGHTING SUCH POWER...

I KNOW IT'S WRONG, BUT PLEASE...! LET ME DO IT MYSELF...!!

BUT NEXT TIME... I SWEAR I'M GONNA SURPASS HIM... GONNA BEAT HIM...!!

I GUESS IT'S MY SAIYAN BLOOD... IT'S NOT SMART, I KNOW...

17

.....

....
BUT..........

HFF

TONG...

NEXT TIME, YOU BETTER KICK HIS BUTT!!

BUT LISTEN, GOKU...!

YOU SAVED THE EARTH...I GUESS YOU'VE GOT THE RIGHT...TO HAVE IT YOUR WAY...

HEH!!

YEAH...!

18

HEHH... THERE WON'T BE... ANY MIRACLES...

N... NEXT TIME, LITTLE BOYS...

H-HAVE FUN...WHILE YOU CAN...

VNN---N

T··M

YOU.... STINKING........

T-TMP

T-TMP

IT'S OKAY, GOHAN... IT'S OKAY...

...HE'S GONE...?

H-HE'S...

HE DIDN'T FINISH HIM OFF...?!

CAN'T BELIEVE THAT IDIOT...

NEXT: *Momma's Coming*

The Bittersweet End

VWOOO----ON

PSSHHH

GOHAN
!!!!

WOPP

VNN--N

CHI-
CHI...
!

BOING

VOOM

UH-OH...

.....

WHAT DID THEY DO TO YOU?!!!

WAKE UP, BABY!!! WAKE UP!!! MOMMY'S HERE!!!

GOHAN !!!

GOHAN !!!

...YOUR HUSBAND...?

...UM... CHI-CHI...?

I'LL NEVER DO IT AGAIN !!!

I'M SORRY I LEFT YOU WITH HIM!!!

SPEAK TO ME

G-GOHAN'S JUST FINE... GOKU'S THE ONE WHO'S REALLY...

24

OOO... THIS LOOKS BAD...

GOKU... ARE YOU OKAY...?

T-TMP T-TMP

THE SAIYAN... GOT AWAY... S...SORRY....

B-BULMA... THEY GOT EVERYBODY BUT US FOUR... INCLUDING YAMCHA...

THERE'S NO WORD FOR POWER LIKE HIS...

DO NOT BE SORRY FOR SUCH A VICTORY.

...OH... MASTER KARIN...

RIGHT?

•••••

I-I'M RIGHT, RIGHT...?!

UM...

WE'LL USE THE DRAGON BALLS IN A YEAR...

I FIGURED THAT. BUT IT'S OKAY!

AND THEY'LL COME BACK TO LIFE!

OH C-COME ON...! YOU'RE JOKING, RIGHT...?!!

Y-YOU SAID FOUR SURVIVED...! S-SO TH-THE OTHER ONE'S GOTTA BE PICCOLO, RIGHT?!

PICCOLO IS DEAD... AND SO...

THE DRAGON BALLS... ARE GONE...

YAMCHA... YAMCHA'S NEVER... NEVER.....?!

N...NO... YOU DON'T MEAN...

•••••

hmph

OH, IT DOES, DOES IT?

YOU KNEW...?

WELL... YES...

WAAAAAH!!!

B... BUT...

26

I JUST ASSUMED... THAT PICCOLO SURVIVED TOO...

I CAN'T BELIEVE IT...

THESE PEOPLE NEED MEDICAL ATTENTION.

ENOUGH. ENOUGH.

AND I HAVE NO MORE "SENZU" BEANS.

IF I HADN'T BEEN HERE, THESE GUYS'D ALL BE DEAD !!!

WOULD A LITTLE THANK YOU HURT?!

WAIT A MINUTE!! I ALMOST GET THE FEELING YOU WISH IT WAS *ME* WHO GOT IT!!

CAREFUL. CAREFUL.

...N...!

27

I KNOW THIS IS REALLY UNLIKELY...

BULMA... PLEASE DON'T CRY...

I MEAN, IT'S A REALLY SLIM CHANCE...

A... A LITTLE MORE THAT WAY...

AND THE... BODIES OF THE OTHERS...?

hic SOB

...THAT WE CAN BRING THEM BACK TO LIFE...

I DON'T WANT TO GET YOUR HOPES UP YET... BUT I THINK THERE MIGHT, MAYBE, BE A POSSIBILITY...

OF COURSE, I COULD BE GRASPING AT STRAWS....

WHAT ?!

HANG ON, I'LL TELL YOU LATER.

WHOA !

DOWN THERE, MASTER... THAT'S WHERE THE BODIES ARE...

YOU SAID.... SOMETHING LIKE THAT BEFORE..... WHAT IS IT, KURIRIN...? TELL US WHAT....

THERE.... ISN'T ONE... H-HE... BLEW HIMSELF TO BITS...

BUT... WHERE IS CHAOZU'S BODY..... ?!

WHAT A TERRIBLE TASK....

GO HAVE A GOOD CRY! IT DID WONDERS FOR ME!

I FEEL SUCH RAGE AT MY HELP-LESSNESS...

I DO WISH WE COULD BRING THEM BACK TO LIFE. THEIR SACRIFICES HAVE BEEN SO GREAT...

VOOOOOOSH

OH
!!!

YOU'RE
AWAKE
?!

GO-
HAN
!!

M...
MM...

...M...

OHHH, YOU
POOR BAAAAABY!!
YOU MUST'VE
BEEN SO
SCAAAARED...!!

M-
MOMMY...
!!

IT'S
ALL RIGHT,
SWEET-
HEART!
MOMMA'S
HERE!

W...
WHAT...
?!

HE...

UH....

GOT
AWAY...
!

B-BUT
THE
SAIYAN...
?!

IT'S
OVER,
GOHAN
!

HE
FOUGHT
WELL. YOU
SHOULD BE
PROUD.

I
BET HE
NEVER
COMES
BACK
!

BUT WE
REALLY
TOOK IT
OUT OF
HIM!

I'LL BE FINE.... THANKS TO ALL OF YOU...!

BEHIND YOU, GOHAN...

 WH-WHERE'S DADDY...?!

 SAVE IT FOR LATER!!

HOW MUCH YOU WANNA--

.....

 SHOW A LITTLE CONCERN, WILL YA?

HEY, AREN'T YOU THE WIFE?

WHAT KINDA MARRIAGE IS THIS?

 HEH HEH...

DADDY...!

 KURIRIN...

SAY WHAT YOU WERE ABOUT TO SAY....

 GOKU, CAN I HIT HER?

OH, WHAT DO I CARE ABOUT THE EARTH?!

B-BUT MOM... THE WHOLE EARTH WAS...

 CONCERN?! AFTER HE NEARLY GOT HIS OWN SON KILLED?!!

I'VE TOLD HIM NOT TO DRAG MY BABY INTO--

32

R-RIGHT.... IT'S JUST...

...OH...!

REALLY...?

!?

...THE SAIYANS... I THINK... FOUND OUT ABOUT THE DRAGON BALLS...AND THEIR WISH-GRANTING POWERS...THROUGH GOKU'S BROTHER'S TRANSMITTER...

BUT... THEY SAID SOMETHING WEIRD WHEN THEY SAW PICCOLO..."HE'S A NAMEKIAN!" THEY MADE IT SOUND LIKE PICCOLO... AND KAMI-SAMA TOO...WERE ORIGINALLY ALIENS...

YEAH...

THEN THEY SAID SOMETHING ELSE...

LET HIM SPEAK!!

WITH FACES LIKE THOSE, WHO'S SURPRISED?!

...SO THEY WERE TRYING TO GET THE DRAGON BALLS WHILE THEY WERE HERE...

"IF WE DON'T GET THEM HERE...WE SHOULD JUST GO THERE..."

I'M NOT SURE... BUT IT WAS SOMETHING LIKE, "SO IT'S TRUE THAT THERE ARE GLOBES THAT GRANT WISHES ON THE PLANET NAMEK"...

THAT'S THE BIG SECRET?

PFFT.

WE MIGHT BE ABLE TO FIND DRAGON BALLS...

IF... IF WE COULD GET TO THIS PLANET NAMEK...

I...I THINK I HEARD THAT TOO....

...AND THEN EVERYONE WHO DIED COULD BE RESTORED TO LIFE...!!

I DID!! NAMEKIANS HAVE POWERS TO MAKE MAGIC BALLS...!!

34

AND OUR DRAGON BALLS WOULD COME BACK TOO!

THAT'S RIGHT! AND IF PICCOLO CAME BACK TO LIFE, SO WOULD KAMI-SAMA...!!

G-GOHAN, WHAT ARE YOU SAYING ?!!

PICCOLO WOULD COME BACK TO LIFE TOO!!

ANOTHER PLANET...? IT'S FANTASTIC...IT'S IMPOSSIBLE.....

Y'MEAN... THAT'S YOUR ONE HOPE... ?

OH, COME ON, BULMA!

IT COULD WORK!! IT REALLY COULD!!

HA HA HA!!

OH...

KURIRIN... HOW ARE YOU EVEN GOING TO FIND OUT WHERE THIS WHAT'S-IT PLANET IS?

I HAVE A FEELING HE'LL KNOW...

LEAVE IT TO ME...I CAN CONTACT THE LORD OF WORLDS THROUGH MY MIND...

NEXT: All Aboard...for Planet Namek!

VOOONNNN

WHY DO YOU THINK THEY CALL ME THE LORD OF WORLDS?

PLANET NAMEK? OF COURSE I KNOW.

KAIŌ-SAMA... YOU WERE LISTENING. DO YOU KNOW...

...WHERE THIS PLANET NAMEK IS?

H-H-HEY... I CAN HEAR HIM TOO?!

OKAY. THIS IS A TRICK... ISN'T IT?

!!

WHEN SON GOKU WENT DOWN, I HONESTLY THOUGHT IT WAS OVER. I'M IMPRESSED, REALLY!

FIRST, LET ME SAY ONE THING... YOU DID VERY WELL!

THEY'RE ALL LISTENING. TELL US, PLEASE.

LORD OF WORLDS...

ACTUALLY, A PRETTY BIG MISCALCULATION...

WELL...*AHEM*... YES. VEGETA'S POWER WAS A BIT OF A MISCALCULATION ON MY PART AS WELL.

NOT EVEN THE KAIŌ-KEN DID MUCH AGAINST HIM.

I DIDN'T EXPECT HIM TO BE SO POWERFUL.

NOW, ABOUT NAMEK'S POSITION... IN EARTH TERMS, LET'S SEE... IT'S BEARING SUB3... 9045YX...

YOU DO THAT.

WHOA, WHOA, WHOA! YOU DON'T MEAN GOKU DID IT ON PURPOSE?!

I'LL... UH...TELL YOU ABOUT IT LATER...

D-DID I MAKE A MISTAKE... IN LETTING HIM ESCAPE...?

...WELL... FRANKLY...

"TURTLE BOY"...?

HEY, TURTLE BOY, TAKE OVER FOR ME! I'VE GOTTA DO SOME CALCULATIONS...!

DON'T TELL ME YOU KNOW WHAT THAT MEANS, BULMA?!

N-9045... YX...!

...THE PLANET DOES SEEM TO BE GOING BACK TO THE WAY IT USED TO BE...

PLANET NAMEK WAS ONCE A PARADISE... BUT, IF I'M NOT CONFUSING IT WITH SOME OTHER PLACE, IT SUFFERED A CLIMATIC CATACLYSM LONG AGO... ACTUALLY, I THOUGHT THE NAMEKIANS ALL DIED OFF AT THE TIME... *HMM*...

BUT HOW COULD ANY OF THEM HAVE SURVIVED...?

I HAVE A BAD FEELING ABOUT THIS...

pi pi pi piiiiii

I'LL JUST HAVE TO CHECK UP ON THE PLANET...

NOW, NOW. DON'T JUMP TO CONCLUSIONS.

...WHICH WAY IS IT AGAIN...?

Y'MEAN IT'S NO GOOD?! THERE WON'T BE NO DRAGON BALLS?!

OHHH, NO...

...BUT THEN FORGOTTEN IT HIMSELF, EITHER BECAUSE HE WAS TOO YOUNG, OR HE LOST HIS MEMORY IN THE TRAUMA... WHAT A TRAGEDY...

I SEE. THEN KAMI... OR I SHOULD SAY THE NAMEKIAN WHO CALLS HIMSELF THAT... MUST HAVE ESCAPED THE CATACLYSM...

LET'S SEE...

AH! THIS WAY!

.....

...THAT HE COULDN'T GRANT A WISH THAT SURPASSED THE POWERS OF THE CREATOR OF THE DRAGON BALLS. WHATEVER CAUSED THE CATA*CLYSM* WAS TOO MUCH FOR THE NAMEKIANS.

UH-UH. IMPOSSIBLE. WE GOT IT STRAIGHT FROM THE DRAGON GOD'S MOUTH...

WHICH, INCIDENTALLY, IS WHY SHENLONG COULDN'T DO ANYTHING ABOUT THE SAIYANS EITHER.

SO IF THE NAMEKIANS COULD MAKE THOSE THINGS, HOW COME THEY COULDN'T USE 'EM TO STOP THE CATECHISM?!

B-B-BUT DRAGON BALLS GRANT ANY WISH, RIGHT?!

THERE ARE ONLY ABOUT A HUNDRED OF THEM... BUT THEY'VE SURVIVED... AND THEY'RE THRIVING AGAIN!!

OH, DEAR L-- I MEAN, DEAR *ME!!* THEY'RE *THERE!* THE NAMEKIANS ARE *THERE!!*

AND I THOUGHT DRAGON BALLS WERE SUPPOSED TO BE SO HOT!

WHAT A CROCK!

GACK! A H-H-HUNDRED OF THOSE GUYS...?

Y E S !!!

!!

DON'T WORRY. NAMEKIANS ARE A MOSTLY PEACEFUL RACE...JUST LIKE KAMI-SAMA OF EARTH WAS. THE GREAT DEMON PICCOLO WAS MOST LIKELY CORRUPTED BY THE MALICIOUS HUMANS HE MET ALONG THE WAY...

HANG ON...DOES THIS MEAN THAT NOT ONLY KAMI-SAMA COULD RETURN TO LIFE... BUT YAMCHA AND TENSHINHAN COULD TOO?!

LOOK WHO'S TALKING...

YEAH. I GUESS THERE'S BAD IN EVERY RACE...EVEN HUMANS.

BUT IT WON'T GO AS EASY AS THAT!

I ADMIRE YOUR OPTIMISM...

40

H-HOW...? W-WITH A SPACESHIP, OF COURSE...

WE KNOW WHERE PLANET NAMEK IS. BUT HOW ARE WE GOING TO GET THERE?

HUH ?!

I CALCULATED THE TIME IT WOULD TAKE TO REACH NAMEK ON A SPACE-SHIP WITH THE FASTEST ENGINE MY DAD'S MADE... WHICH WOULD BE THE FASTEST IN THE WORLD.

THAT'S PRECISELY WHAT I'M SAYING!

LORD OF WORLDS...

WHAT SHOULD WE DO...?

F-F-FOUR... THOUSAND... ?!

TRY 4339 YEARS AND 3 MONTHS !!

HOPE NOBODY'S IN A HURRY...

ANY-BODY WANT TO TAKE A GUESS? NO?

THAT'S AN AWFULLY GOOD QUESTION...

WELL... HMM... UH...

WHAT'S EVERY-BODY SO SAD ABOUT ?!

HEH HEH !

SHHHH

BUT... VEGETA ESCAPED IN IT...

THE SAIYANS'...?

LET'S JUST USE THE SAIYANS' SPACE-SHIPS !

?

YEAH. IN A LITTLE TINY SHIP THAT HADDA BE FOR *ONE!* THAT MEANS HIS DEAD BUDDY'S SHIP MUST STILL BE SOMEWHERE!

IF WE CAN FIND IT AND ANALYZE IT, MAYBE WE CAN USE IT!!

BUT THERE'S AT LEAST ONE, THEN!

EXCEPT... THAT ONE WAS BROKEN...

BY GOHAN...

YEAH! YEAH! THERE WAS THE ONE MY BROTHER CAME ON, TOO...!

I THINK IT'S WHAT VEGETA PRESSED TO CALL HIS SPACESHIP! MUST BE SOME KINDA REMOTE CONTROL!

I THOUGHT IT'D BE USEFUL, SO I PICKED THIS UP....

LET'S GO LOOK FOR IT, RIGHT NOW!

IT'S PROBABLY AT THE EASTERN CITY... THE FIRST PLACE THE SAIYANS DESTROYED!

HOPE, AT LAST!!!

HA HA HA!!!

YES!!!

W-WE CAN DO IT! WE CAN DO IT!

HEH HEH... HEH HEH...

WELL, THAT'S NOT EXACTLY WHAT I WANTED TO HEAR. FOUR MONTHS FOR MY INJURIES TO HEAL, THEY SAID!

AND I MIGHT *NEVER* GET BACK TO NORMAL...

IN ANOTHER MONTH THERE'LL BE SOME NEW SENZU ON ITS TREE.

OH, THERE'S NOTHING TO WORRY ABOUT.

LEAST WE DON'T HAVE TO PLAY MUMMY, LIKE YOU.

GOHAN AND I'LL BE OKAY WITH JUST THREE DAYS IN THE HOSPITAL. LUCKY, I GUESS.

WE **KONG HOSPITAL**

44

BEGGING THE SAIYAN TO FORGIVE YOU AND LET YOU JOIN THEIR GANG?

AFTER YOU WENT THROUGH ALL *WHAT*, YAJIROBE?

OR DID I DREAM THAT?

ARE YOU THAT DESPERATE FOR HOSPITAL FOOD?

I WENT THROUGH ALL THAT AND I DON'T EVEN GET TO BE HOSPITALIZED!

HMPH...

YOU SAVED THE EARTH. YOU SURVIVED. AND MAYBE THOSE WHO DIED CAN RETURN TO LIFE TOO. IT'S ENOUGH.

FORGET IT, FORGET IT.

THAT WAS JUST A STRAJATEM TO TRICK 'EM!

YA WANNA GET BEAT UP, BALDY?!

AH, YOUR "STRAJATEMS"!

EVERY-BODY CHECK OUT WHAT'S ON TV!!

HEY!!

45

46

A BLIP HERE... A BEEP THERE...

JUST WATCH! WE'LL BE ABLE TO SEE IT ON LIVE TV!

KURIRIN. WHO'S THE GENIUS IN THIS ROOM?

I CHECKED OUT ALL THE CONTROLS LAST NIGHT!

DO YOU THINK IT'LL ACTUALLY WORK...?

I CAN'T SEE!!

GULP

AND WATCH THAT THING MOVE!

HUH ?!

DOOM

SOMETHING'S HAPPENED...! THE OBJECT...IT'S SUDDENLY EXPLODED!! THE REMAINS OF THE SPACECRAFT, IF SUCH IT WAS, ARE SCATTERED EVERYWHERE...!

IS NOW TOTALLY SUNK.

THE... THE LAST HOPE...

I TOLD MYSELF, "DON'T TOUCH THE SELF-DESTRUCT BUTTON"!

OHHHH, SHOOT!!!

IT'S ALL OVER...

IT'S...

NOT EVEN KINTO'UN... COULD CARRY US FAST ENOUGH...

THERE'S... THERE'S NOTHING TO DO...

YOU HAD TO PICK UP THAT STUPID REMOTE CONTROL!

YOU HAD TO PRESS THE STUPID SELF-DESTRUCT BUTTON!

WEST KONG ✚ HOSPITAL

48

EXCUSE MR. POPO.

WAAH!!!

INDEED.

MR. PUH-PUH-PUH---

EEEP!!

HUH ?!

THERE IS A SPACE-SHIP.

SOME-ONE COME.

NEXT: What Th'?!

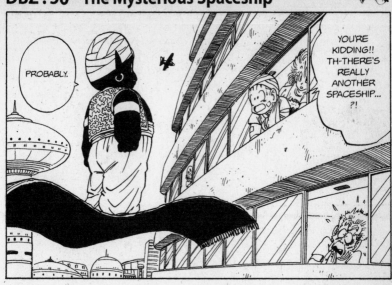

PROBABLY.

YOU'RE KIDDING!! TH-THERE'S REALLY ANOTHER SPACESHIP...?!

BACK UP, BACK UP. "PROBABLY"...?

AND SAYS HE HAS SINCE BEFORE THE CURRENT KAMI-SAMA AND THE ONE BEFORE THAT AND THE ONE BEFORE THAT....

HE LIVES AT KAMI-SAMA'S CASTLE.

IT'S MR. POPO.

WHO'S THIS GUY?

IF SOME-ONE COMES, MR. POPO WILL GUIDE HIM.

PROBABLY A SPACESHIP. BUT MR. POPO CANNOT BE SURE.

DON'T YOU THINK THIS GUY HAS KINDA SHIFTY EYES...?

I-I-I DON'T KNOW ABOUT THIS...

WHO ELSE COULD FIGURE OUT AN ALIEN SPACESHIP?

BULMA!

ME?!

SLOWLY, SLOWLY!!

MR. POPO IS OFF.

WELL...JUST BE CAREFUL!! I'M NOT LIKE THEM-- I'M A DELICATE LI'L GIRLIE!

YOU CAN'T CHICKEN OUT ON US NOW, BULMA!!

HOSPITAL

IF THERE'S REALLY A SPACESHIP... WHOSE IS IT?

UM...I DON'T SUPPOSE ANYONE KNOWS HOW HE DID THAT...

VNNNN

51

Y-YOU MEAN TO TELL ME THAT IN THAT INSTANT...

THAT'S THE FARTHEST CORNER OF THE EARTH!!

NOW, LET MR. POPO SEE....

YUNZABIT HIGHLANDS.

Y-YUNZABIT...?!

DRAG THE LUSCIOUS BABE OUT WHERE NOBODY CAN SEE WHAT YOU'RE GONNA DO TO HER, EH?!

OH, I GET IT...

WHOA! WAIT! TIME OUT!

WAS IT THIS WAY?

YOU EXPECT ME TO BELIEVE THERE'S A SPACESHIP IN A PLACE LIKE THIS?!

HUH?!

HERE IT IS.

EXACTLY WHAT DO YOU KNOW ABOUT THIS?!

OKAY, ENOUGH O' THE POPO MYSTERY THEATER!

I'VE NEVER SEEN ANYTHING LIKE IT...

WH-WHAT IS THIS...? IT'S NOT METAL...

TONG TONG

IT WAS A MYSTERIOUS TALE. KAMI-SAMA SAID THAT HIS GODSHIP HAD LIVED IN THE YUNZABIT HIGHLANDS AS A CHILD. THEN MR. POPO SAID THAT THE YUNZABIT IS A WASTELAND. WHY WOULD A CHILD BE THERE?

A CENTURY AGO, THE LORD KAMI-SAMA SPOKE OF HIS GODLY PAST TO MR. POPO...FOR THE FIRST AND ONLY TIME.

KAMI-SAMA REPLIED: NO PARENTS. ONLY A NOTE READING, "WE WILL COME FOR YOU LATER." WAIT FOR US..."

MR. POPO ASKED AGAIN: WERE HIS GODSHIP'S PARENTS THERE?

KAMI-SAMA SAID THAT HIS GODSHIP DID NOT KNOW. EVEN HIS LORDLY MIND WAS CONFUSED. PERHAPS THE GODLY HEAD HAD BEEN STRUCK AND HIS HOLY MEMORY LOST....

AND...?

THE LORD KAMI-SAMA WAITED FOR HIS HOLY PARENTS FOR A LONG TIME. AND WAITED AND WAITED....

JUST TELL ME WHERE THIS IS GOING, OKAY ?!

LOOK, I'M NOT GOOD AT SUSPENSEFUL NARRATIVES !

BUT THE YEARS STRETCHED ON... AND NO ONE CAME. IT WAS HARD... FINDING FOOD WAS HARD...

THERE WAS A HOUSE THERE... I TRUSTED THAT MY PARENTS WOULD COME... SOMEDAY...

MORTALS ARE SO IMPATIENT. MR. POPO COMES TO THE POINT...

UM...DID I FORGET TO ASK... WHERE'S THIS **GOING** ?!

FINALLY, I GAVE UP AND LEFT THE HOUSE... AND YUNZABIT...

HOW LONG DID I WAIT? 20 YEARS? 30?

I DIDN'T KNOW ANY OTHER HOUSES, AFTER ALL...

IT DIDN'T OCCUR TO ME AT THE TIME...

I RETURNED THERE FROM TIME TO TIME TO SEE IF THERE WAS ANY SIGN... BUT NOTHING CHANGED...

IT WAS ROUND AND HAD 4 LEGS... VERY MUCH LIKE SOME SORT OF CREATURE... THERE WAS NO KNOB OR LOCK ON THE DOOR, AND IT OPENED WITH A SPOKEN WORD...

BUT AS I CAME TO KNOW DIFFERENT WORLDS, I REALIZED WHAT AN ODD HOUSE THAT WAS.

PPPP--!!

"PICCOLO."

GO IN.

THEN THIS-- THIS---!!

57

SAY IT AGAIN, AND IT CLOSES. "PICCOLO."

TH-THIS IS KAMI-SAMA'S HOUSE...!!

LOOK CAREFULLY. IS THIS A HOUSE? OR A SPACE-SHIP?

SLAM

!!

THE LORD OF WORLDS TOLD US THAT!! AND ABOUT A CATACLYSM THAT DESTROYED NAMEK A LONG TIME AGO!

OF COURSE!! KAMI-SAMA WAS A NAMEKIAN...!!

58

I-IF THIS IS A SPACESHIP, THEN HIS STORY MAKES TOTAL SENSE...!

MR. POPO THOUGHT THAT PERHAPS IT WAS WORTH TAKING A LOOK FOR THIS HOUSE...

MR. POPO ALSO HEARD THE LORD OF WORLDS SPEAK. THEN MR. POPO REMEMBERED THE STORY ABOUT THIS HOUSE.

'CAUSE I NEVER SAW ANY HOUSE LIKE THIS!

THAT'S GOTTA BE IT!

IT'S GOTTA BE A SHIP...!

FOR SOME REASON THEY COULDN'T COME UNTIL LATER... AND THEN SOMETHING WENT WRONG... THEY...THEY NEVER MADE IT....

WHEN PLANET NAMEK WAS IN DANGER, KAMI-SAMA'S HOLY PARENTS PUT HIS GODSHIP ON BOARD AND FLEW HIM TO EARTH...

IS THIS... THE MAIN SWITCH? NO...

THE DOOR'S WORKING, SO THERE MUST BE SOME POWER...

UM... THIS ONE IS...

B-BUT... HOW DO WE USE IT...?

HMM... THAT'S NOT IT EITHER...

YEAH! IF IT WAS TOO EASY TO WORK, KAMI-SAMA WOULD'VE MESSED WITH IT WHEN HE WAS LITTLE!

THIS IS WEIRD... I WONDER IF THERE'S A PASSCODE OR SOME-THING...

YEAH!! WORDS! LIKE THE ENTRANCE!!

VOICE SENSORS?

BUT WHAT ARE THEY? SOME KINDA SENSOR?

I... DON'T THINK THESE ARE BUTTONS...

!!

SHH�art-HH

MOVE!! CAN YOU HEAR ME?! FLY!!

ZOOM!! LIFT!! ZIP!! TRAVEL!!

NO! THAT'S GOTTA BE JUST TO GET IN AND OUT!

WHAT TO SAY? "PICCOLO"?

...THEN MR. POPO KNOWS IT!

IF THAT WAS NAMEKIAN...

KAMI-SAMA AND PICCOLO WERE TALKING IN SOME STRANGE LANGUAGE AT THE MARTIAL ARTS TOURNAMENT...

THAT MUST'VE BEEN NAMEKIAN.

IT'S NO USE... IT WOULDN'T BE IN AN EARTH LANGUAGE. TOO BAD NOBODY KNOWS NAMEKIAN...

OH, WHO CARES?! WHY DIDN'T YOU TELL ME YOU SPOKE NAMEKIAN?!

SO THE GREAT DEMON PICCOLO MEANS....

REALLY.

NOW THAT MR. POPO THINKS ABOUT IT, "PICCOLO" IS A PERFECT ENTRANCE WORD. IT MEANS "DIFFERENT WORLD" IN THAT LANGUAGE.

REALLY ?!!

ᚥᚤᚢ ᚦᚤᚡᚢ ᚦ.ᚦᚥᚤᚡ ᚤ!

TO WHERE?

WHEREVER! FOR STARTERS, HOW 'BOUT... AROUND JUPITER!

AND WHY DON'T YOU TELL THIS THING TO *FLY*?!

IT SAYS "ROGER" !!

!!

piiii

AAAA!!!

VOOOONN

GYNNNNN

CAPS

62

.....

NNNNN

YES.
YES,
INDEED.

WE DID IT !!!!

I HOPE YOU DON'T THINK I'M BEING PREMATURE IN SAYING....

YYYYYYYYUP....
THAT'S JUPITER, ALL RIGHT!

NOW KAMI-SAMA MAY COME BACK TO LIFE...

MR. POPO IS GLAD.

NEXT: *Take-off!!*

WITH THAT, WE CAN GET TO PLANET NAMEK IN JUST ONE MONTH! WE'LL JUST HAVE TO REVAMP THE INTERIOR A LITTLE...

...AND SO THE SPACESHIP IS PERFECT!!

THAT IS RIGHT.

AND WE CAN TAKE OFF IN 5 DAYS!!

CAPSULE CORPORATION

WEST KONG + HOSPITAL

DBZ:51 • 3...2...1...Lift Off!

HUH?

SO, MR. POPO, WE'LL LEAVE GOING TO PLANET NAMEK TO YOU!!

MR. POPO ISN'T GOING.

THE FAINT GLIMMER OF HOPE IS ABOUT TO BECOME REALITY!

GOING TO PLANET NAMEK ON KAMI-SAMA'S SHIP!! THAT'S AWESOME!!

64

DON'T WORRY, MR. POPO WILL TEACH NAMEKIAN.

MR. POPO CAN'T GO. THERE WOULD BE NOBODY AT KAMI-SAMA'S CASTLE FOR 2 MONTHS; NO GOOD.

YOU'RE THE ONLY ONE WHO UNDERSTANDS NAMEKIAN!! AND YOU LOOK TOUGH!! THE ONLY WAY IS FOR YOU TO GO!!

WHAT?! B-BUT!!

...I'LL HAVE TO ADD A SHOWER ROOM... A MORE COMFORTABLE BED, AND A STEREO...

...A-ALL RIGHT... IT DOESN'T SOUND TOO DANGEROUS...

MUMBLE MUMBLE

YOU'RE THE ONLY ONE KNOWLEDGEABLE ABOUT MECHANICS IF SOMETHING GOES WRONG.

THEN YOU WOULD HAVE TO GO, BULMA.

NOBODY EXPECTED YOU TO.

YOU'RE NOT GOING TO GET ME TO GO!!

BUT I DON'T WANT TO GO ALONE! SOMEONE COME WITH ME!

KURIRIN! YOU'LL COME WITH ME, WON'T YOU?!

SON'S IN NO SHAPE...

THAT'LL JUST ADD NEEDLESS DANGER!!

2 MONTHS ROUND TRIP... ALL RIGHT! OH WELL, I'LL GO!

65

I WANTED TO SEE WHAT PLANET NAMEK'S SHENLONG LOOKED LIKE...

LUCKY YOU. I WANT TO GO TOO.

W-WELL, ALL RIGHT... 2 MONTHS... I'D WANTED TO TRAIN...

WHAT? M-ME?

WE DON'T KNOW WHEN THE SAIYAN IS COMING BACK...

WITH YOU...! PLEASE...

T-TAKE ME

YEAH... WE'RE COUNTING ON YOU TWO.

WELL, YOU TAKE IT EASY AND WORK OUT COUNTER-MEASURES AGAINST THE SAIYAN.

WH-WHAT KIND OF SILLY JOKE ARE YOU MAKING...?

G-GOHAN...

I-I SERIOUSLY WANT TO GO.

IT'S NOT A JOKE.

I'M SORRY... I... WANT TO GO, NO MATTER WHAT... I WANT TO... BRING PICCOLO BACK TO LIFE WITH MY OWN HANDS...

D-DON'T BE RIDICULOUS... T-TWO MONTHS, ON TOP OF ALL THIS...

B-BEST KEEP AWAY...

THERE'S NO NEED FOR GOHAN TO DO THAT!! WHAT IF SOMETHING WERE TO HAPPEN?!

WHAT KIND OF NONSENSE ARE YOU TWO TALKING ABOUT ?!!

GOOD FOR YOU, GOHAN.

...I SEE.

...

YOU'RE A LITTLE KID!! YOU SHOULD ACT LIKE ONE!!

WHO CARES ABOUT PICCOLO ?!

WHAT ABOUT CRAM SCHOOL?! YOUR LESSONS?! YOU'RE WAY BEHIND ALL THE OTHER KIDS ALREADY !!

2 MONTHS!! AFTER AN ENTIRE YEAR OF WORRYING !!

I WON'T ALLOW IT, I ABSOLUTELY FORBID IT!!!

BE QUIET !!!!

H-HAS BECOME A DELINQUENT...

M-MY LITTLE BOY...

EVERYONE... WE ALL FOUGHT FOR THE EARTH... WE HAVE TO BRING THOSE WHO DIED BACK TO LIFE... AND FIGHT THE SAIYAN AGAIN...

M-MOM... NOW... NOW'S NOT THE TIME TO BE SAYING SUCH THINGS...

LET GOHAN FLY INTO SPACE WITH YOUR BLESSING.

YOU LOSE, CHI-CHI...

HEE HEE. THAT KID SAYS GOOD STUFF SOME- TIMES.

I CAN... I CAN FIGHT TOO...!

I HAVE TO DO SOME- THING... !!

68

LET'S SEE NOW... WE'LL RE-INPUT THE NAMEKIAN LANGUAGE... AND MEET AT THE TURTLE HOUSE IN 10 DAYS!!

IT'LL BE FINE! LEAVE IT TO US; THERE'S NOTHING DANGEROUS!

I'M PROUD OF YOU. YOU'VE GOTTEN SO STRONG...

GOHAN...

DON'T JUST BE IMPRESSED; HELP ME, DAD!

THIS IS REALLY AMAZING! THE UNIVERSE IS VAST. I GUESS THERE ARE SMARTER GENIUSES THAN ME.

AND FINALLY, THE DAY OF DEPARTURE...

AREN'T YOU UNDERESTIMATING OUTER SPACE...? I EVEN CUT MY HAIR BECAUSE IT WOULD GET IN THE WAY OF MY SPACESUIT...

K-KURIRIN, WHAT A NICE OUTFIT YOU HAVE...

MUMBLE GRUMBLE

HUH ?

B-BULMA, CAN WE REALLY GO INTO SPACE IN THIS THING?

WOW...

70

SAY BULMA, SHOULD WE TAKE AN UMBRELLA? PLANET NAMEK MIGHT NOT HAVE GOOD WEATHER, RIGHT?

WHATEVER YOU WANT.

OH, HE CALLED TO SAY THAT HE WAS GOING TO SEE GOKU, AND THEN COME RIGHT OVER.

...AND WHERE'S GOHAN?

BYOOO--

OH! LOOKS LIKE THEY'RE HERE!

HOO-WHEE. SO THIS IS A SPACE-SHIP! AMAZING!

NOW THEN GOHAN, BE CAREFUL!

SORRY WE'RE A LITTLE LATE!

THUD

BE SURE TO BRUSH YOUR TEETH AFTER MEALS!

O-OK...

YOU'RE GOING INTO SPACE WHERE NO MAN HAS GONE BEFORE. YOU'LL HAVE TO BE ON YOUR BEST BEHAVIOR.

WHAT'S WITH YOUR HEAD?

HA HA HA HA!! A-ARE YOU REALLY GOHAN?!

D-DAD LAUGHED AT ME TOO...

I FEEL WASHED OUT...

W-WE BETTER GET GOING...

72

GOHAN, DON'T FORGET TO SHAMPOO *AND* CONDITION YOUR HAIR!!

WH-WHAT SPEED! I-I CAN'T SEE THEM ANYMORE!

B-BULMA, WE HAVEN'T F-FASTENED OUR SEAT-BELTS YET!!

ONCE WE'RE OUT OF THE ATMOSPHERE, IT'S QUIET.

HMPH! YOU'RE FREE TO MOVE AROUND NOW.

HUH?! A-ALREADY ?!

WHOOSH

75

HUH? CHANGE... INTO YOUR PAJAMAS? YOU'RE GOING TO SLEEP ALREADY?

LEAVE ME ALONE, I'M GOING TO CHANGE!

HEY, WHERE ARE YOU GOING, BULMA...?

I WANTED TO SEE EARTH.

THIS...

HEH HEH...

IN THOSE SUNDAY-SCHOOL CLOTHES THIS WHOLE TIME?

BY THE WAY, ARE YOU REALLY GOING TO STAY

SLAM

YES! ABOUT THE SAME AS DAD.

YOU MUST REALLY RESPECT PICCOLO...

NO, ACTUALLY, I MADE SOME CLOTHES WITHOUT TELLING MOM...

OH SHOOT... COME TO THINK OF IT, I FORGOT MY PAJAMAS... WHAT ABOUT YOU, GOHAN?

I BROUGHT MINE.

THEY LOOK UNCOMFORTABLE TO SLEEP IN...

HUH...? WH-WHAT STRANGE PAJAMAS...

TUMP

LOOKING AT YOU, I STARTED TO FEEL RIDICULOUS FOR HAVING SO ENTHUSIASTICALLY PREPARED FOR OUTER SPACE!

OF COURSE THEY'RE NOT PAJAMAS!!

HO HO HO!!

NOT KNOWING THE TERROR THAT AWAITED THEM...

AND SO THE 3 TOOK OFF TO PLANET NAMEK...

DID WE DO SOMETHING WRONG...?

S-SAY...

I-I DON'T KNOW...

NEXT: *Vegeta Returns!*

IT MUST BE THERE! SEEKING THE NEW DRAGON BALLS, BULMA, KURIRIN, AND SON GOHAN SET OUT TO PLANET NAMEK, THE HOME OF PICCOLO AND KAMI-SAMA. HOWEVER...

I'M BORED TO DEATH...

SIGH...

YAWWN...

ARE YOU GUYS IMAGE-TRAINING AGAIN...?

YOU'RE LUCKY YOU CAN KILL TIME LIKE THAT...

OH GEEZ... IT'S STILL ONLY THE 7TH DAY... 20-PLUS DAYS TO GO...

I SHOULD'VE MADE SOME STASIS CHAMBERS OR SOMETHING.

...UNH...!

BUT I WAS SURPRISED AT THE NUMBER OF MOVES YOU HAVE!

AFTER ALL, YOU'RE DESCENDED FROM GOKU AND YOU WERE TRAINED BY PICCOLO...

YOU'RE GOOD! YOU REALLY ARE STRONG.

HUFF HUFF...

AH!

WE CLEANED UP OUR OWN TRASH ALREADY...

B-BUT YOU'RE THE ONE WHO MADE THE MESS OVER THERE...

...BUT THIS PLACE HAS GOTTEN PRETTY MESSY, SO COULD YOU CLEAN IT UP?

SAY, TRAINING IN YOUR MIND IS ALL WELL AND GOOD...

ALL YOU GUYS HAVE TO DO IS JUST SIT ON BOARD.

I'M BUSY! THERE'S LOTS OF STUFF I HAVE TO THINK ABOUT.

THERE'S A LADY IN HERE!

IF SHE'S A LADY, I WISH SHE WOULDN'T WANDER AROUND IN HER UNDERWEAR...

• • •

BUSY BUSY!

SHUT UP! CAN'T YOU BE CONSIDERATE TO A DELICATE LADY...?

I THOUGHT YOU SAID YOU WERE BORED...

I MEAN, THEIR PLANET'S LONG GONE, RIGHT?

HUH? WHERE...?

I'D BEEN WONDERING ABOUT THAT SAIYAN WHO GOT AWAY, VEGETA.

BY THE WAY...

WHERE'D HE RUN *TO?*

80

I WONDER IF HE'S GETTING TREATED BY THOSE ALIENS...

HMM... SON-KUN'S BROTHER SAID ONCE... "WE LOCATE HOSPITABLE PLANETS AND SELL THEM TO OTHER RACES LOOKING FOR LIVING SPACE."

SO I'D THINK IT WOULD BE SOME PLANET WITH CIVILIZATION...

...OH YEAH... IN ANY CASE, HE ALSO TOOK A LOT OF DAMAGE...

...EARTH HAS SURE GOTTEN MARKED BY AN UNBELIEVABLE GUY...

WE'D HAVE MORE TIME IF IT WERE FAR AWAY...

IF THAT'S THE CASE, HOW SOON HE COMES BACK TO EARTH WOULD DEPEND ON WHERE THAT PLANET IS...

BULMA'S CONJECTURES WERE NOT WRONG AT ALL...

WHOOO

PLANET FREEZA NO. 79... ON THE 18TH DAY AFTER VEGETA LEFT EARTH...

82

THIS SIGNAL... IT'S LORD VEGETA!!

ROUND-TYPE! IT'S A COMBATANT!

IT COULDN'T BE!! HE JUST WENT OUT!

IS IT LORD FREEZA?!

HYEEEEE

ODD! WE HADN'T BEEN INFORMED OF HIS RETURN!

DID SOMETHING HAPPEN?!

HEY!! THIS IS CONTROL!! LORD VEGETA IS ARRIVING!! SOMEONE RECEIVE HIM AT ONCE!!

HERE HE COMES !!!

IT *IS* JUST ONE POD, WHERE'S NAPPA?!

Ten-HUT!

84

WH-WHAT'S THE MATTER...?! HE'S NOT COMING OUT...

H-HEY, HIS LIFE SIGNS ARE AWFULLY WEAK!!

...?

TH-THIS IS BAD!! TAKE HIM TO THE TREATMENT CENTER, NOW!!!

HE'S USING LIFE SUP-PORT !!

SHHK

GLUG GLUG

BLUP BLOOP

ALL RIGHT.

YOU'RE ALL HEALED. YOU MAY OPEN YOUR EYES NOW.

WHIIII

UNFORTUNATELY, YOUR TAIL COULD NOT BE REGENERATED...

NO MATTER, IT'LL GROW BACK AGAIN.

IS LORD FREEZA IN?

NO, HE HAS GONE OUT...

YOU MUST'VE HAD A HARD TIME EVEN WITH YOUR GREAT STRENGTH... TO THINK THAT THIS SUPER-QUALITY RUBBER ARMOR WAS DESTROYED...

TELL HIM THAT I HAVE NOTHING TO SAY TO HIM.

HAH!

LORD KIWI SAID FOR YOU TO COME TO THE TRAINING ROOM AFTER YOUR TREATMENT, AS HE HAD TO TALK TO YOU...

HE'S TIRED OF THIS PLANET ALREADY...

HMPH...!

OH...! YOU FORGOT YOUR SCOUTER...

WHAT?

I DON'T NEED IT. IT'S YOURS.

87

!

I'LL DESTROY THEM THIS TIME FOR SURE...!

I'LL HEAD TO EARTH FIRST THING TOMORROW MORNING...!

I HEARD YOU WENT THROUGH HELL. *HEH HEH HEH...*

YO, VEGETA!

I HEARD THAT RADITZ AND NAPPA DIED TOO. *HEH HEH HEH...* WHO COULD'VE TORMENTED THE SUPPOSEDLY INVINCIBLE SAIYANS THUS?

NO... I SHOULD GO TO PLANET NAMEK FIRST...

I-I HAVE TO BEAT HIM THERE, OR I'LL HAVE TO DO HIS BIDDING FOREVER...!!

ARGGHH! HE LISTENED TO OUR CONVERSATION THROUGH THE SCOUTERS... I SHOULD'VE KNOWN BETTER...!

DASH

THAT ROT-TEN...!!

HEY, VEGETA!!

LORD FREEZA IS PLANNING TO ANNIHILATE THE NAMEKIANS ONCE HE GETS HIS WISH.

UNH...!

I HEAR THAT YOU HAD WANTED ETERNAL LIFE WITH THESE DRAGON BALLS TOO, BUT GIVE IT UP. HA HA HA!

VEGETA!!

WHOOSH

THOSE DRAGON BALLS ARE *MINE* !!!

HE'S NOT GOING TO GET AWAY WITH THAT...!!

WE DID IT!!! THERE IT IS!!

AND ON THE 34TH DAY AFTER LEAVING EARTH... BULMA AND CO. FINALLY ARRIVED AT THEIR DESTINATION, PLANET NAMEK...

NEXT: Planetfall

DRAGON BALL

ドラゴンボール

DBZ : 53

**Planet Namek,
Cold and Dark**

FASTEN YOUR SEATBELTS, WE'RE IN FOR A BUMPY LANDING!

OKAY !

THAT'S *IF* WE CAN FIND A PLACE TO LAND AT ALL......!

Piii

HYUUUUUUN

WHOA !!

UN- BELIEV- ABLE !!

SO THAT'S PLANET NAMEK !

WOW! IT'S PRETTY !

WOW!!

WE DID IT!! WE'VE LANDED ON PLANET NAMEK!!

YEEP!!

I BROUGHT OXYGEN MASKS JUST IN CASE, BUT OUR TIME OUTSIDE'D BE AWFULLY LIMITED....

piip piip

NOW, IF THERE'S JUST ANY AMOUNT OF OXYGEN...

I'LL CHECK THE ATMO-SPHERIC COMPO-SITION.

HANG ON...

LUCKILY I WAS SMART ENOUGH TO ATTACH EXTERNAL SENSORS!

YEAH... THE PLACE WHERE WE FIRST FOUGHT THE SAIYANS, RIGHT? PIC PROB'LY INSTINCTIVELY FELT BETTER IN A PLACE THAT LOOKED LIKE "HOME"...

THIS... LOOKS A LITTLE LIKE THE PLACE WHERE PICCOLO TRAINED ME...

95

OH, YEAH, WHY DON'T YOU FELLOWS JUST STROLL ON OUT?! DID YOU BRING LAWN CHAIRS?!!!

MAYBE SHE'S JEALOUS 'CAUSE WE GOT OFF FIRST...

I-I DON'T KNOW...

HUH? WHAT'S SHE MAD ABOUT THIS TIME?!

SHEESH...!! LET'S JUST START LOOKING FOR THE DRAGON BALLS!!!

Piii

!?

CHK CHK

WE HAVE A READING...!! THERE **ARE** DRAGON BALLS HERE!!!

LOOK!!

YOU'RE RIGHT!!!!

WE DID IT! WE DID IT! WOO HOO!!

Y-YOU'RE RIGHT...!!

...

CHI?

THERE'S SOME STRONG **CHI** THAT WAY...

KURIRIN...

WH-WHAT COULD IT BE...?

AND EVERY ONE OF 'EM'S STRONG...

Y-YEAH...

I FEEL A LOT OF THEM...

YEAH... EVIL, THAT'S WHAT THEY ARE....

B-BUT... THEY'RE...

IF KAMI-SAMA AND PICCOLO WERE AS STRONG AS THEY WERE, THEN OF COURSE *REAL* NAMEKIANS ARE GONNA HAVE AMAZING CHI-POWER!

DUH! WHAT DO YOU EXPECT? THOSE ARE NAMEKIANS!

IT'S ONLY THE NAMEKIANS!

Y-YEAH! OF...OF COURSE!

OH, COME ON! THE LORD OF WORLDS HIMSELF SAID THE NAMEKIANS ARE GENTLE AND PEACEFUL AND...

AND LOOK! ISN'T THAT EXACTLY WHERE THE RADAR'S SHOWING FOUR BALLS GROUPED TOGETHER?

HA! YOU GUYS'LL WORRY ABOUT ANY-THING!

SO LET'S GO MEET THESE NAMEKIANS!

HA HA..

KIII~IIN

KIII~IIN

HUH ?!

99

IT'S THE SAIYAN'S SPACESHIP !!!!

N-N-NO !!!

I CAN'T BELIEVE THIS...! WHY WOULD...?!

IT'S VEGETA...! IT HAS TO BE...!!

R-RIGHT!!!

GOHAN!!! SUPPRESS YOUR CHI!!! HE'LL SENSE YOU!!!

NO!! I KNOW WHAT WE'RE GOING TO DO!! WE'RE GOING BACK TO EARTH!! NOW!!!

WH-WH-WHAT ARE WE GOING TO DO...?!

DID THE SAIYAN... G-GET HEALED ALREADY...?

DON'T YOU REMEMBER? HE WAS LOOKING FOR THE DRAGON BALLS TOO!

FUMP

PWAP

BULMA, YOU GO BACK TO EARTH BY YOURSELF....

BUT IF HE GETS AHOLD OF THOSE DRAGON BALLS...

IT'LL BE ALL RIGHT... WE HAVE THE DRAGON RADAR...

WE'LL STAY-- AND WE'LL GET THOSE DRAGON BALLS!

101

ONCE I REACH EARTH, I'LL GRAB GOKU AND COME BACK! IT'LL BE A LITTLE OVER TWO MONTHS ROUND TRIP... WAIT FOR US!

OKAY! FIRST I'LL SEND A WARNING TO THE TURTLE HERMIT....

Y-YEAH!!!

...RIGHT, GOHAN...?

T-TWO MONTHS... RIGHT....

THE DRAGON BALLS... ARE MINE...!!

THAT STINKING FREEZA...

102

I DIDN'T THINK I'D HAVE TO USE THE SCOUTERS AGAIN...

HMPH...

I FEAR NO ONE ELSE...BUT FREEZA IS ANOTHER MATTER...

THEY MUST HAVE LEARNED ABOUT MY REBELLION BY NOW...FREEZA WILL WANT ME DEAD...

I'LL HAVE TO TAKE THE DRAGON BALLS SOMEHOW... AND ATTAIN IMMORTALITY.

HE'S BROUGHT ZARBON AND DODORIA WITH HIM AS WELL...!!

THIS WAY!

pi pi pi!

HE WHAT...?!

...UH-HUH... UH-HUH...

Y-YOU SAW *WHO*?!

103

HM?

THANKS! BYE!

EXCEPT... WHATEVER YOU DO, DON'T TELL CHI-CHI!

GOT IT?! NOW TELL THAT TO GOKU! AND EVERYBODY!

HUH? WHAT...?!

H-HOW COULD THAT...!!

HUH?!

H-HEY...

...

KIII—IIN

IT IS OURS, LORD FREEZA!!

NOW WE HAVE THREE LEFT TO GO.

THANK YOU.

YES, SIR!

I HEAR THAT VEGETA IS AFTER THEM...

LOOK AFTER IT WELL, DEAR DODORIA.

KIWI WILL DISPATCH HIM SOON ENOUGH. THOSE TWO ALWAYS DID HATE EACH OTHER.

FINE, FINE. BUT OUR PRIORITY IS THE REBELLIOUS VEGETA.

LORD FREEZA, KIWI HAS ARRIVED JUST NOW, PURSUING VEGETA. THE TWO LARGE POWER READINGS THAT SUDDENLY APPEARED AND DISAPPEARED HAVEN'T YET RETURNED.

THEIR ABILITIES ARE BASICALLY EQUAL, WHICH SHOULD AT LEAST STOP VEGETA FROM TAKING THE DRAGON BALL!

WE'RE IN-VESTIGATING THE AREA OF THE READINGS. WITH LUCK, WE'LL SOON KNOW WHAT THEY WERE.

I'LL SEE TO THAT MYSELF...!

YOU WON'T GET AWAY, VEGETA!

NEXT: The Welcoming Party!

TH-THERE SHOULDN'T BE ANY MORE SAIYANS... WHO *WAS* THAT...?!

O---KAY... SO HOW DO WE GET OUT OF *THIS* MESS?!!

HEH HEH HEH... I'VE GOT YOU, VEGETA...

piii pi pi pi

DO YOU HEAR ME, VEGETA?! AT LAST I CAN KILL YOU !!!!

AND THE ORDERS I'VE WANTED FROM LORD FREEZA !!

HWAH!

DO YOU REALLY THINK YOU CAN KILL ME?

DON'T MAKE ME LAUGH, KIWI.

I'LL WAIT FOR YOU. DON'T DAWDLE.

MY COMBAT POWER IS WELL ABOVE YOURS!

HAAH HA HA! ARE YOU BLIND?! LOOK AT YOUR SCOUTER!!

I'LL BE RIGHT BACK-- IN TWO MONTHS!!

WELL THEN...I'M OFF TO EARTH!! GOOD LUCK!!

HEH!

109

M-MAYBE WE SHOULD GO BACK TO EARTH TOO, FOR A WHILE?

G-GOHAN, WH-WHAT SHOULD WE DO ...?

HUH?

BULMA... WAIT A MINUTE...!!

W-WELL, YEAH... F-FOR NOW! THEN WHEN WE COME B-BACK WE CAN TAKE 'IM ON AGAIN AN'--

BUT THEN... WOULDN'T HE GET THE DRAGON BALLS...?

I-I MEAN, I'M FINE, N-NO PROBLEM...BUT IF ANYTHING BAD HAPPENED TO Y-YOU....!!

I-IT L-LOOKS LIKE THERE'S MORE THAN ONE ENEMY...

...BUT...

...

IF SHENLONG DOESN'T GET KILLED FIRST, LIKE LAST TIME WITH PICCOLO...

HUH?!

KURIRIN, SOMEONE'S COMING!!

IT SHOULD BE AROUND HERE THAT THE READING BROKE OFF...

PROBABLY JUST A NAMEKIAN....

NO... IT'S NOT VEGETA... IT'S A MUCH WEAKER *CHI*...

I-IS IT A SAIYAN ?!

WHAT IS THAT?!

HUH ?!

IT'S PR-PROBABLY A NAMEKIAN...

GULP...

TH-THEY'RE NOT NAMEKIANS !!!

HUH ?!

OUR ORDERS ARE TO KILL EVERYONE ON THIS PLANET...

HEH HEH HEH, IT DOESN'T MATTER.

THEY DON'T LOOK NAMEKIAN. WHO ARE THEY?

I-I DUNNO WHAT'S GOING ON... BUT I GOT A BAD FEELING...

...BUT THEY'RE NOT SAIYANS...

L-LOOK AT THEIR CLOTHES... THEY'RE THE SAME AS WHAT THE SAIYANS WERE WEARING...

WHATEVER THEY'RE WEARING... THEY DON'T LOOK LIKE THEY WANT TO MAKE FRIENDS...!

Y-Y-YEAH...

112

GOHAN-- SUPPRESS YOUR CHI AND CONCENTRATE IT!

O- OKAY.

FWOOo

!?

ALL RIGHT !

!?

HA! DID YOU SEE THAT? THEY HAVE PRACTICALLY NO COMBAT POWER. THEY MUST BE TOURISTS!

pi pi pi

HEH HEH HEH... IT'LL BE NO FUN IF THEY RUN. DO THE SPACESHIP FIRST.

BOOM

EEK!!!

ZIIII

SSSS...

TH- THE SPACE- SHIP!!!

GACK!!!!

RELEASE YOUR CHI!

GOHAN-- THESE GUYS ARE NOTHING!

YIP...!

HAAH HA HA!!

BAD LUCK, LITTLE TOURISTS!! YOU SHOULD HAVE COME LAST WEEK!!

114

YEAH!!!

LET'S GO!!!

HA HA HA! YEAH, WE'RE "NOTHING"-- JUST LIKE *DEATH!*

HEY, DID YOU HEAR THAT?

pi pi pi pi

HUH?!

TH-THIS POWER LEVEL-- IT'S TOO HIGH!!

WH-WHAT IS THIS...?!

ZWOOOM

NO--
!!

SHHP

SHHP

FP

FP

BLO OSH

BLO OSH

TP

TP

HWRRRRR

IT WAS *NOT*!!!

THAT WAS NICE!

HEY!

PHEW.

Piiii

118

IT APPEARS WE'RE FACING MORE THAN ORDINARY BEINGS. THEIR POWER INDICES ROSE SHARPLY FOR A MOMENT, AND AFTER DEFEATING OUR SCOUTS, DISAPPEARED AGAIN...

LORD FREEZA... CONCERNING THE RECONNAISSANCE WE SENT OUT EARLIER...

WHAT IS THE TROUBLE, LOYAL ZARBON?

I SEE.

THEIR POWERS WERE BOTH ABOUT 1500.

THE READING IS QUITE DIFFERENT FROM VEGETA'S.

THAT IS ODD. IT DOES NOT SOUND LIKE VEGETA...

I WOULD LIKE TO LEARN MORE ABOUT THEM, BUT CIRCUMSTANCES DO NOT GIVE US THE LUXURY.

1500...

IF YOU FIND THEM AGAIN, ELIMINATE THEM.

THERE M-MIGHT BE STRONGER GUYS C-COMING... WE GOTTA GO!

B-BULMA... W-WE'RE IN DANGER HERE....

WE CAN NEVER GET BACK TO EARTH!

IT'S...IT'S NO USE... IT'S ALL OVER...

hic
SOB

WE CAN'T LET THEM FIND US...

I GUESS THE *CHI* WE FELT WASN'T NAMEKIANS...IT WAS VEGETA'S PEOPLE...

I'M SURE THE NAMEKIANS WILL FIX THE SHIP...

W-WE GOTTA HIDE SOME-WHERE...

SIGH
I WISH I HAD YOUR YOUTHFUL OPTIMISM...

IT APPEARS THE TIME HAS FINALLY COME FOR US TO SETTLE THE SCORE...

HEH HEH HEH... SO, VEGETA...

SOMETHING INTERESTING I LEARNED WHEN I WENT TO EARTH...

HAVEN'T I...? WELL THEN, I'LL HAVE TO SHOW YOU MY NEW DISCOVERY...

YOU'VE BEEN SLACKING OFF... WITH THAT POWER LEVEL, YOU HAVE NO CHANCE.

HEH

NO. HOW TO CONCEAL MY *TRUE* POWER !!!!

HOW TO RUN AWAY QUICKLY ?

FEH !

NEXT: The True Power!

YOU CAN... CONCEAL YOUR POWER LEVEL?!

pipipi..!!

Y-YOUR POWER...IS SUPPOSED TO BE THE SAME AS MINE...!!

I-IMPOS-SIBLE...!!

WATCH MY COMBAT POWER NUMBER CLOSELY ON YOUR SCOUTER!!

FOOL!! I'VE BEEN FIGHTING CONTINUOUSLY-- IN *REAL* BATTLES!! ON EARTH I NEARLY DIED!!!

HOW CAN YOU KEEP UP WITH ME, SNUGGLING SAFE AND SOUND AT FREEZA'S?!

122

...

WHAT'S THE MATTER, ZARBON?!

BOOM

!!

I'LL GET THE CORRECT NUMBER OFF MINE...

IT **HAS** TO BE A MALFUNCTION! YOUR SCOUTER'S A LEMON!

BUT THE POWER-COUNTER SET TO VEGETA... J-JUST WENT PAST 22,000...!

I-IT'S PROBABLY A MAL-FUNCTION...

pipi pipi pi..!!

TH-THIS CAN'T BE RIGHT... I-I'VE GOT THE NEWEST SCOUTER ON THE MARKET! IT CAN'T BE **24,000**!!!

AND THE CORRECT NUMBER...?

TWUH...?!

IT'S IMPOSSIBLE !!

24,000?! THAT'S HIGHER THAN *OURS!!*

VEGETA COULD BARELY GET UP TO 18,000!

AND SURELY 24,000 IS NOT BEYOND YOUR OWN IMPRESSIVE POWERS...IF YOU FIGHT *TOGETHER.* HEH...

WHY SO SURPRISED? VEGETA HAS LONG BEEN IN THE FRONT LINES, AFTER ALL. HE MUST HAVE LEARNED SOMETHING NEW WHILE ON EARTH.

STILL, IT IS RASH OF HIM... HEH-HEH...

HE WOULD NOT HAVE A CHANCE AGAINST ME OTHERWISE. *SIGH* WE'VE BEEN ON THIS PATH TO CONFLICT SINCE THE BEGINNING, IT SEEMS...

I SUPPOSE VEGETA DESIRES THE SAME WISH OF THE DRAGON BALLS AS DO I... ETERNAL LIFE.

...TO REBEL OPENLY AGAINST ME...

HE WENT TO EARTH WITHOUT BEING ORDERED. HE SEEKS POWER FOR HIMSELF. NOW IT SEEMS HE COVETS MY POSITION.

...

...

L-LET ME JOIN YOU!! HOW ABOUT IT?! I CAN HELP YOU OUT!!

W-WAIT, VEGETA! I JUST THOUGHT OF SOMETHING!

I'VE SECRETLY HATED THE MAS--I MEAN, *FREEZA*--FOR A LONG TIME MYSELF!!

BUT YOU'RE A *LYING* COWARD TOO!

AND HERE I THOUGHT YOU WERE JUST A COWARD, KIWI...

N-NOT BAD, EH?! WITH OUR POWERS COMBINED, WE COULD TAKE OUT ZARBON AND DODORIA LIKE NOTHING!

OH!! MASTER FREEZA !!!

WHAT ?!

TRUST ME, VEGETA...

LYING?! M-ME ?!

...

GNNG

HEH...
HEH
HEH
HEH...

NOT YOUR ETHICS. BUT YOUR PATHETIC ATTEMPT AT **STRATEGY**.

YOU DISAPPOINT ME, KIWI.

I DON'T CARE **HOW** STRONG YOU ARE--YOU'RE NOTHING IF YOU LEAVE YOURSELF WIDE OPEN!!

HA-HA-**HA**! BETTER A LIAR THAN A FOOL !

IF MY POWER INCREASES... DOESN'T MY SPEED INCREASE ALONG WITH IT?

B-B-BUT I JUST... !!!

AND MY **RAGE**, KIWI. MY **RAGE** INCREASES WITH EACH OF YOUR STUPID ASSAULTS.

128

IT'S OVER, KIWI !!!!

UNH !!!

FWAA

...

VNNN

VNNN

KRII

!!!

HOOOSH

HEH!!

I CAN HANDLE ZARBON AND DODORIA, BUT IF I APPROACH TOO RECKLESSLY...

FREEZA'S MEN WILL BE FOLLOWING ME WITH THEIR SCOUTERS...

I'D HAVE NO CHANCE AGAINST FREEZA.

TP

I'VE ALWAYS LOVED FIRE-WORKS!

AH !

ALL RIGHT, THEN. I'LL FIND ONE OF THEM. ONCE THEY'VE FOUND THE OTHER SIX, I'LL LOOK FOR AN OPENING AND TAKE THEM FOR MYSELF.

ACCORDING TO WHAT I OVERHEARD THROUGH THE SCOUTER, THE DRAGON BALLS HAVE NO EFFECT UNLESS YOU'VE GATHERED ALL SEVEN TOGETHER.

VEGETA, THE SAIYAN, WILL RULE THE UNIVERSE !!!!

ONCE HE'S GONE, I WILL STAND SUPREME!!

IF THAT GOES WELL... ETERNAL LIFE WILL BE MINE...

AND DEFEATING FREEZA WILL NO LONGER BE A DREAM!

...HE SWATTED KIWI LIKE A FLY...

TH-THEN HIS POWER LEVEL REALLY *IS*... 24,000...

I HAVE A READING OF TEN OR SO NAMEKIANS IN THAT DIRECTION.

EXCELLENT. LET'S HOPE THEY HAVE THE DRAGON BALL, MM?

NO MATTER.

THERE APPEAR TO BE OTHER STRANGE BEINGS OUT THERE...

IN THE MEANTIME, LET NONE OF US LET DOWN HIS GUARD.

LET US BE OFF!

YES, MASTER.

LET US GO LOOK FOR THE FIFTH DRAGON BALL, SHALL WE?

YOU GUYS CAN FLY, CAN'T YOU?! SO CARRY ME!!

HUF PUF

BULMA, CAN'T YOU GO ANY FASTER?! WE'RE SITTING DUCKS OUT HERE!

HEY! BULMA, LOOK OVER THERE!

WE'LL BE HARD TO SPOT IN THAT CAVE!

IT TAKES SO MUCH *CHI* TO FLY, THE BAD GUYS'D FIND US IF WE USED IT!

I WISH I COULD...BUT I CAN'T IF I'M GOING TO HIDE MY *CHI*...

SOB

hic

HUH?

KURIRIN... DO YOU FEEL SOME CHI THAT WAY?!

Y-YOU'RE RIGHT...!

B-BUT HOW LONG...

...

W-WILL WE HAVE TO ST-STAY THERE...?!

THEY COULD BE NAMEKIANS THIS TIME...

FEELS DIFFERENT FROM THE GUYS WE RAN INTO EARLIER...

THERE'S ANOTHER STRANGE CHI COMING RIGHT AT US!

HIDE!!!

NEXT: Goku to the Rescue!...Sort of !

YOU TOO, BULMA-- HIDE!!! IT'S THE FRIENDS OF THE GUYS WE FOUGHT EARLIER!!!!

HUH ?!

D-DO YOU TH-THINK THEY SPOTTED US...?

SHUT UP! THEY'RE COMING THIS WAY!

Y'KNOW, I'VE BEEN MEANING TO ASK HOW YOU TWO CAN TELL THESE THINGS...

KIIIIIN

THEY WENT BY SO FAST I COULDN'T SEE...

BUT... WHAT WERE THEY, ANYWAY?

I GUESS WE WEREN'T WHAT THEY WERE AFTER!!

TH-THEY'RE GONE...

TH-THERE WERE FOUR DRAGON BALLS... CL-CLUSTERED IN A GROUP... S-SEE IF THOSE GUYS WERE THE ONES WHO HAD 'EM...

B-BULMA...? C-COULD YOU CONFIRM SOMETHING ON THE D-DRAGON RADAR...?

CONFIRM WHAT...?

KURIRIN

BRRRR...

KURIRIN, WHAT'S WRONG...?

HUF

HUF

HUF

138

THEY WERE CARRYING FOUR DRAGON BALLS!!

YEAH!! NO DOUBT ABOUT IT!!

pii

pii

CHK CHK

Y-YEAH...

GOHAN... DID YOU SEE...? TH-THE WEIRD GUY FLYING SECOND FROM THE LEAD...

I... SAW HIM...

...?

I KNEW IT...

KAMESEN KURIRIN

AND I FELT... HIS POWER...

KAMESEN KURIRIN

THE OTHERS WERE SOMETHIN', TOO... B-BUT *HE*...!

ME TOO. AND I *FROZE.* THAT LITTLE SQUIRT...COULD BE A LOT MORE POWERFUL THAN VEGETA...!

HOW ARE WE S'POSED TO GET THE DRAGON BALLS AWAY FROM *THOSE* MONSTERS?

DAM-MIT...

I DON'T KNOW! B-BUT JUDGIN' BY THE CLOTHES, I'D SAY TH-THEY'RE ALL WITH VEGETA...

S-STRONGER... THAN VEGETA?! B-BUT WHO... WHO...?

WH-WHERE IS THIS...?

WHAT'S GOING ON?! DO THEY HAVE THEIR OWN RADAR...?

THEY'RE HEADING STRAIGHT TOWARDS THIS *OTHER* DRAGON BALL...!

LOOK...!

H-HEY!

CHK CHK

I'M... G-GONNA GO THERE AND CHECK IT OUT...!

THAT'S WHERE WE FELT THE CHI YOU SAID MIGHT BE NAMEKIANS...

ABOUT... 14KM IN THAT DIRECTION...

I'LL GO WITH YOU!

YEAH.

140

THEN REPORT THIS TO MASTER MUTEN-RŌSHI, OKAY?

W-WELL... Y-YEAH...

OKAY. I'LL PUT UP A CAPSULE HOUSE INSIDE THE CAVE AND WAIT HERE.

...

I THINK IT'S A LOT SAFER *HERE*...

W-WAIT A MINUTE!! YOU'RE NOT GONNA LEAVE ME HERE ALL *ALONE*?!

YEAH!

YOU THINK YOU CAN DO IT?

GOHAN, WE'VE GOTTA HURRY--BUT SUPPRESS OUR CHI AS MUCH AS WE CAN!

W-WILL DO. B-BE CAREFUL!

SHH SHHAAA

SHHHPP

141

WHERE'S YOUR WIFE?

SHOPPING. SAID SHE WAS BORED...

S-SORRY...

I DON'T BELIEVE YOUR NONSENSE ABOUT FIGHTING ALIENS...BUT FOR WHATEVER REASON, YOU'RE IN SERIOUS CONDITION.

UM... CHI-CHI'S NOT HERE?

SHE WENT OUT FOR A WHILE.

OH DOCTOR, HOW DO YOU DO?

HOW'S IT GOING, GOKU?

EEEEK!

DID THEY GET TO PLANET NAMEK ALL RIGHT?

GOKU... I RECEIVED WORD FROM BULMA ABOUT TWO HOURS AGO...

PAT PAT

THANKS!

PERFECT...

HERE'S SOME GET-WELL POUND CAKE FOR YOU. HAVE SOME.

143

UNFORTUNATELY...

YES, THEY REACHED NAMEK WITHOUT PROBLEMS...

HM? DID I DO SOMETHING JUST NOW?

...

I MUST BE GETTING OLD. I DO THINGS WITHOUT REALIZING IT THESE DAYS...

BUT... BUT THEN...

VEGETA ?!

IT SEEMS THAT VEGETA... WENT THERE TOO...!

THEY WEREN'T THE ONLY ONES WHO WENT TO THAT PLANET...

...VEGETA HAS AT LEAST TEN COMRADES ON NAMEK. THEY DESTROYED OUR GROUP'S SPACESHIP... AND NOW THEY'RE STRANDED THERE!

LISTEN TO ME. THE TURTLE JUST RADIOED ME... HE'S JUST RECEIVED NEW INFORMATION FROM BULMA, AND ACCORDING TO HIM...

...N- NO... NO !!

AND... AT LEAST ONE OF THE TEN... HAS A CHI SURPASSING EVEN VEGETA'S...

WH- WHAT... ?!

144

WHAT? I THOUGHT YOU'D BE ALL HAPPY TO SEE ME!

YOU ALIVE, MONKEY MAN?

'EY, YO!

KARIN TOLD ME TO BRING YOU ALL SEVEN!

SOME SENZU ARE FINALLY DONE. JUST A FEW THOUGH.

AAAH

HERE YOU GO.

H-HEY!! WHAT ARE YOU FEEDING TO MY PATIENT?!

GIVE ME ONE! NOW!!

REALLY?! WHAT PERFECT TIMING!!

HEH

GL LL LP

MMF MMF

145

T-TO PLANET NAMEK... B-BUT HOW?!

THANKS, I'LL TAKE THE REST OF THEM!

NAMEK, HERE I COME!!

ALL RIGHT!!

...TO MAKE ME A SPACESHIP JUST IN CASE!

HEH HEH... WHEN BULMA'S DAD CAME TO SEE ME, I ASKED HIM...

THE ONE MY BROTHER CAME ON...

I THOUGHT REAL HARD...AND REMEMBERED THAT TWO SAIYAN SPACESHIPS HAD COME TO EARTH *BEFORE* VEGETA AND NAPPA!

AND THE ONE I CAME ON WHEN I WAS A KID!

TH-THEN...?

NO, NO. THAT USED SOME ALIEN MATERIALS SO EVEN HE COULDN'T COPY IT.

I SEE! THE SAME AS KAMI-SAMA'S?

I CAN GET TO PLANET NAMEK IN 6 DAYS!

WITH THAT...

I HAD BULMA'S DAD GO LOOK FOR IT.

TH- THAT'S RIGHT !!

MY BROTHER'S HAD EXPLODED, BUT MINE WAS AN OLDER MODEL SO IT WAS SAFE! I HAD HIM FIX IT UP!

EEEEK !!!

WELL, I'M OFF TO SAVE 'EM!!

VWA

KINTO'UN !!!

TO BULMA'S HOUSE !!

HYUUUN

TP

148

WHY'S HE LOOK SO *JAZZED* WHEN SOMETHING SO HORRIBLE IS HAPPENING?!

W H A T ?!

...HIS SON AND HIS TWO OLDEST FRIENDS...

W-WELL...

SAVE... WHO?

...

HE DOES WANT TO SAVE THEM... BUT PART OF HIM JUST *LOVES* GOING UP AGAINST POWERFUL OPPONENTS...!

I CAN ONLY THINK IT'S THE SAIYAN BLOOD...

I MEAN, HE'S OBVIOUSLY GOT NO CHANCE...

I DON'T KNOW WHETHER TO ADMIRE THE GUY OR PITY HIM...

FIGHTERS EVEN STRONGER THAN VEGETA!

I CAN'T BELIEVE IT!

NEXT: *Son Goku's Spaceship*

ONE BEAN FROM MASTER KARIN'S "SENZU" PLANT... AND GOKU'S INJURIES WERE MAGICALLY HEALED.

NOW, HAVING LEARNED OF THE CRISIS THAT HIS SON AND FRIENDS ARE FACING ON PLANET NAMEK, GOKU RUSHES TO BULMA'S HOUSE TO FIND THE SAIYAN SPACESHIP THAT HE'D EARLIER WANTED RESTORED...JUST IN CASE...

CAPSULE CORP.

DBZ:57 • Son Goku's Spaceship

TMP

HE'S GOT TO BE DONE!

HMUN

INSIDE THE HOUSE?

WHERE WOULD HE HAVE IT...?

MY MY MY! YOU'RE LOOKING SO WELL!

GOOD AS NEW!

... BULMA'S MOM!

OH MY! IS THAT GOKU...?!

Y-YOU MEAN HE HASN'T...?!

WHAT?!

WELL...I THINK I SAW HIM STILL PUTTERING ON IT... MAYBE WE SHOULD TAKE A LOOK...

IS BULMA'S DAD DONE REBUILDING THAT SPACE-SHIP LIKE I ASKED...?

OH, BY THE WAY! I FOUND THIS *DELICIOUS* PASTRY SHOP THE OTHER DAY! AND IT'S ALL THANKS TO YOU! AFTER ALL, I WOULDN'T HAVE BEEN ABLE TO FIND IT IF EARTH HAD BEEN DESTROYED!

HA HA..

...

I CAN'T BELIEVE THAT PUNY LITTLE GOKU GREW UP TO BE SO *CHARMING*!

WE SHOULD GO OUT FOR DRINKS... AFTER YOU BEAT UP THOSE SAIYANS!

IS THIS IT?!

IS...

HUH?

DEAR! LITTLE GOKU'S HERE!

BETTER ALREADY, EH? THOSE SENZU SURE ARE SOMETHING!

THIS... THIS IS THE SPACE-SHIP?!

OH, HEY!

IT'S NOT FINISHED YET?!

152

UH.. TH-THANKS.

I'LL BRING SOMETHING TO DRINK. I'LL CALL PU'AR AND OOLONG OVER WHILE I'M AT IT.

COME ON IN AND TAKE A LOOK.

OH, ALMOST, ALMOST...

WHAT DO YOU THINK? EVERY-THING'S JUST LIKE YOU WANTED IT!

HOW DID THAT TINY SPACESHIP GET SO BIG?

WOW, IT'S HUGE!

THAT SAIYAN TECHNOLOGY SURE IS AMAZING.

I'VE BEEN WORKING HARD. HAD TO REBUILD ALMOST THE WHOLE THING.

I COULD TRAIN ALL I WANT IN HERE.

THIS IS THE SWITCH FOR ARTIFICIAL GRAVITY... AND THIS IS THE CONTROLLER. IT USES THE SPACE-SHIP'S ACCELERATION. LIKE YOU ASKED, IT CAN GENERATE UP TO A MAXIMUM OF 100G...

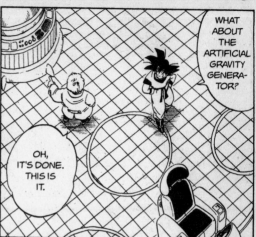

WHAT ABOUT THE ARTIFICIAL GRAVITY GENERA-TOR?

OH, IT'S DONE. THIS IS IT.

IT'S OKAY. IF I COULDN'T HANDLE THAT MUCH I'D NEVER HAVE A CHANCE AGAINST THE SAIYAN.

PROBABLY KILL EVEN YOU.

BUT ISN'T THAT KIND OF EXTREME, EVEN FOR YOU? WITH 100G, IF YOU WEIGH 60 KG YOU BECOME **6000KG!** THAT'S **6 TONS!**

THE BATH, TOILET, KITCHEN, AND BEDROOM ARE DOWN THAT LADDER...

THEN... THEN WHAT ISN'T FINISHED...?!

OH, IT CAN FLY. I'VE INPUT ALL THE DATA, SO ALL YOU HAVE TO DO IS PRESS THE SWITCH AND YOU'LL BE ON NAMEK IN SIX DAYS.

BUT... CAN THIS THING FLY?

154

TH-THAT'S IT?! THAT'S ALL THAT'S NOT FINISHED?!

I MEAN, YOU WANT TO HAVE GOOD SOUND, DON'T YOU?

WELL, I CAN'T DECIDE WHERE TO PUT THE STEREO SPEAKERS...

I'M GOING TO TAKE OFF RIGHT NOW !!!!

I DON'T CARE ABOUT THE STEREO!! I'M IN A HURRY !!

POSITIONING SPEAKERS FOR THE BEST POSSIBLE SOUND IS AN ART FORM, I'LL HAVE YOU KNOW! WHEN YOU CONSIDER THE ACOUSTICS OF...

"THAT'S ALL," HE SAYS !

WELL, THAT *IS* URGENT, ISN'T IT?

MY GOODNESS...!

WHAT COULD BE SO IMPORTANT THAT YOU DON'T CARE ABOUT THE STEREO?

ALL RIGHT! BUT YOU KNOW, ALL I NEED IS A FEW HOURS WITH THE SPEAKERS...

TEACH ME HOW TO FLY THIS THING, NOW!!

I GOT WORD FROM YOUR DAUGHTER--AND MY SON!! THEIR SPACESHIP HAS BEEN *DESTROYED!!* AND THE *SAIYAN* AND HIS GANG ARE ON NAMEK WITH THEM!!

155

156

NOT BAD CONSIDERING HOW FAST I THREW IT TOGETHER!

HMPH!

YEAH. HE WAS IN KIND OF A HURRY.

WAS THAT SOUND WHAT I THINK IT WAS...?

HUH?! WHERE'S GOKU?! WHERE'S THE SPACESHIP?!

I WONDER IF SOMETHING HAPPENED...

I THOUGHT WE WERE FRIENDS... HE COULD'VE AT LEAST SAID HI.

HUH...?

CAPSULE

DA·KOOOM

DOESN'T MATTER. I BETTER START TRAINING!

IT'S GREAT THAT I CAN GET THERE IN SIX DAYS...BUT THAT'S HARDLY LONG ENOUGH TO GET READY TO FIGHT VEGETA...

VNN VNN

PHEW...! TH-THIS THING SURE IS FAST...!

BOY... OUTER SPACE IS DARK. IS IT NIGHT NOW...?

OOG
!!!

HOOOME

I GUESS I SHOULD START GETTING USED TO 20G FOR NOW...

...LET'S SEE, I HEARD THE LORD OF WORLDS' PLACE HAD GRAVITY OF 10G...

pi piiii

ONE TWO!

ONE TWO!

OHH... *THAT'S*... GRAVITY... !!

RRK !!

DOMP

DOMP

OR I'LL NEVER BE ABLE TO HANDLE THE MULTIPLE STRENGTH KAIŌ-KEN...!

I'LL HAVE TO START RETRAINING FROM THE BASICS...

WHOOSH
WHOOSH

OK
!!

WE'RE GETTING CLOSE!! SUPPRESS YOUR CHI COMPLETELY! WE'VE GOT TO SWITCH TO WALKING!

I'M PICKING UP UNBELIEVABLE CHI...

GULP...

OVER THAT CLIFF...!

PEEK

HEY! TH-THERE ARE HOUSES... THAT LOOK LIKE OUR SPACE-SHIP...!

WH-WHAT ARE THEY DOING...?!

TH-THE OTHERS DON'T MATTER AS MUCH...B-BUT THOSE THREE... ESPECIALLY THE GUY IN THE ROUND THING... TH-THEY HAVE *INCREDIBLY* STRONG CHI...!

HM?

OH...!

L-LOOK AT WHAT THE TWO GUYS ON EACH SIDE ARE CARRYING...! D-DRAGON BALLS!

VSSH

TH-THEY'RE HUGE...!

162

IT'S GONE NOW... IT MUST'VE BEEN A SMALL ANIMAL OR AN INSECT.

I DETECTED A VERY SMALL POWER READING IN THAT DIRECTION...

WHAT IS THE MATTER, MR. DODORIA?

THE REST HAD JUST SLIPPED OUT!

MASTER FREEZA, WE FOUND ONLY FIVE OF THEM!

PHEW...

EESH... TH-THAT WAS CLOSE...!

THEY LOOK JUST LIKE KAMI-SAMA AND PICCOLO...!! TH-THEY'RE NAMEKIANS...!!

OUTSIDE!! *NOW*--IF YOU DON'T WANT TO *DIE!!*

NEXT: *The Kindness of Freeza*

BESIDES, THE ONLY SAIYAN LEFT SHOULD BE VEGETA...

...EXCEPT FOR YOU AND GOKU...

NO... THEY HAVE THE SAME CLOTHES, BUT THEY'RE NOT SAIYANS...

K-KURIRIN... ARE THEY ALL SAIYANS?

WH-WHAT ARE THEY GOING TO DO WITH THOSE NAMEKIANS...?

COME TO THINK OF IT, GOKU'S BROTHER SAID, "WE EXTERMINATE THE NATIVES OF HOSPITABLE PLANETS AND SELL THEM TO ALIENS"...

...MAYBE THEY'RE IN ON THAT TOO...

TH-THEN...

BUT IT DOESN'T LOOK LIKE VEGETA'S HERE... IS HE LOOKING FOR DRAGON BALLS SOMEWHERE ELSE...?!

...

NNH...

WHERE ARE THE OTHERS, BY THE WAY? WE HAD NOTED THAT THERE WERE TEN OF YOU...

I AM CALLED FREEZA. AS YOU CAN SEE, I AM COLLECTING YOUR DRAGON BALLS.

WE WILL HAVE TO KILL YOU.

ARE YOU PLANNING TO REMAIN SILENT?

...

!

ϴᗷ⅄ ᗡᐁᴎᴑ
⅂ᑐᗷΖᗯϴᚅ
......

PLEASE SPEAK IN A TONGUE THAT WE UNDERSTAND, NOT NAMEKIAN. WE KNOW THAT YOU CAN SPEAK OUR LANGUAGE.

TH-THE OTHERS... WENT OUT TO WORK IN THE FIELDS... THE ONLY ONES HERE ARE THE ELDERLY AND THE CHILDREN...

...

...

THERE YOU GO. AS LONG AS YOU CAUSE NO TROUBLE AND ANSWER US, YOU WILL BE PERFECTLY FINE.

I-I DON'T KNOW... I MEAN... WE DON'T HAVE ANYTHING LIKE THAT...!

WHERE IS THE DRAGON BALL? THERE IS ONE HERE, I'M QUITE SURE OF THAT.

NOW. ON TO OTHER QUESTIONS.

HEH HEH HEH...

AH, YES. HE WAS VERY **STUBBORN**, AND WOULD NOT COOPERATE WITH US. SO WE KILLED ANOTHER AS A LESSON...

YES. SOMETHING TO THE EFFECT THAT THESE PEOPLE WILL ONLY HAND OVER THE DRAGON BALLS TO GREAT HEROES.

MY DEAR DODORIA...IF I RECALL, THE SECOND NAMEKIAN WE KILLED SAID SOMETHING QUITE INTERESTING.

WH-WHAT...?!

THE MAKER OF THE DRAGON BALLS WAS THE **GREAT ELDER** OF THIS PLANET... WHO DELEGATED TO SEVEN OTHER ELDERS, DISPERSED OVER THE PLANET, THE GUARDIANSHIP OF EACH OF THE SEVEN BALLS. TO OBTAIN ONE, YOU MUST HAVE A CONTEST OF WITS OR STRENGTH... OR EXPLAIN THE REASON FOR THE WISH YOU DESIRE...

THEN HE TOLD US MANY THINGS.

HOW COULD YOU...?

HOW...

AND ONLY AFTER YOU ARE DEEMED WORTHY BY EACH OF THE SEVEN ELDERS CAN YOU POSSESS THEM ALL.

I TRIED TO DO AS HE SAID, BUT HE SAID HE WOULD NEVER GIVE THE BALL TO ME...

SO I KILLED HIM. WHICH MADE IT QUITE TROUBLESOME LOCATING THE FIRST BALL.

THE OTHER THREE WE OBTAINED EASILY. EVERYONE WAS HAPPY TO OBLIGE.

SO THAT'S HOW IT IS...

I SEE...

THE OTHER ELDERS WOULD *NEVER* GIVE THE DRAGON BALLS TO *YOU!*

YOU KILLED THEM TOO!

"HAPPY TO...!" *LIAR!!*

YES SIR!

MR. ZARBON, PLEASE DEMONSTRATE.

NO, REALLY. THEY OBLIGED QUICKLY WHEN WE DID THIS.

HHH HHH

SHP

DON'T
!!!

MONSTER
!!!!

HWA

GACK
!!!!

173

...GA...

BWOOM

TMP

fap

174

DO YOU FEEL INCLINED TO OBLIGE A LITTLE MORE NOW?

WHAT DO YOU THINK?

H-HOW AWFUL.

I...I CAN'T BELIEVE THEM...

WH...WHY DO YOU WANT THE DRAGON BALLS...? WHAT WILL YOU WISH FOR?

...

OH, A SIMPLE WISH. MERELY ETERNAL LIFE FOR MYSELF.

COULD IT BE...?

MAYBE... THEY'RE NOT IN ON IT WITH VEGETA...

TH-THEN WHAT ABOUT VEGETA...? H-HE WAS ALSO AFTER ETERNAL LIFE...

WH-WHAT...?!

TO A CREATURE LIKE YOU... EVEN IF IT MEANS MY LIFE...

I CANNOT GIVE THE DRAGON BALLS

RATHER THAN MAKE ME HAPPY...

HO HO. SO YOU WOULD CHOOSE DEATH...

SURELY NOT *YOU*... WOULD MURDER CHILDREN...!!

WH-WHAT ?!

PEOPLE ON THIS PLANET REALLY ARE STUBBORN. BUT WOULD YOU BE ABLE TO REMAIN SO STUBBORN...WHEN FACED WITH THE DEATHS OF THOSE CHILDREN?

....!!

UNH... !

176

MASTER FREEZA! LOOK!!

COMBAT POWER... ?!

pi pi pi

HWOOOO

AH !!!

OH... ?!

NEXT: *The Reinforcements!*

TITLE PAGE GALLERY

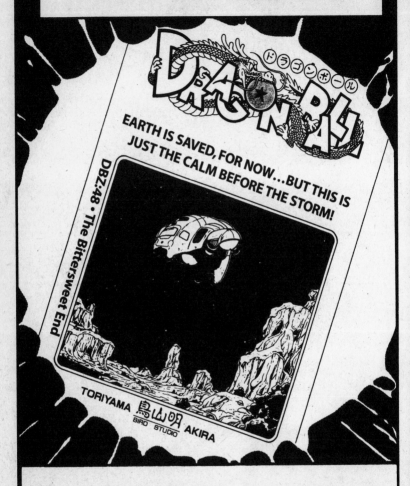

EARTH IS SAVED, FOR NOW...BUT THIS IS JUST THE CALM BEFORE THE STORM!

DBZ:48 • The Bittersweet End

TORIYAMA 鳥山明 AKIRA
BIRD STUDIO

Here are the title pages which were used when these chapters of **Dragon Ball Z** were originally published in Japan in 1990 in **Weekly Shonen Jump** magazine.

ドラゴン ボール

DRAGON BALL

DBZ : 50 • Destination Namek

NEW ADVENTURES WAIT FOR US!!

Akira Toriyama
鳥山明
BIRD STUDIO

ONWARD !!

DRAGON BALL

BALL

WHAT HATH POPO WROUGHT?

Akira Toriyama

BIRD 鳥山明 STUDIO

DRAGON BALL

DBZ : 51 • 3...2...1...Lift Off!

Akira Toriyama

BIRD STUDIO

DBZ:54 The Mysterious Strangers

DRAGON BALL

PLANET NAMEK SPIRALS INTO CHAOS!!!

Akira Toriyama
鳥山明
BIRD STUDIO

DRAGON BALL

Akira Toriyama
鳥山明
BIRD STUDIO

DBZ:55 • Vegeta's True Power!

☆ Who's Who on Planet Namek ☆

Vegeta

Kuririn and the others are aware of Vegeta's presence on Namek, but Vegeta is unaware that they are nearby.

Kuririn

Bulma

Son Gohan

Looking for openings to kill one another.

Have sensed one another's chi, but have not seen one another in the flesh.

Originally one of Freeza's underlings, until he rebelled. He wants to achieve eternal life and defeat Freeza.

Dodoria

The space ship that our heroes used to get to Namek has broken down and can't return to Earth.

Freeza

Zarbon

Freeza's underling. Strong and unpredictable.

Freeza's underling. Very strong.

Son Goku

Still hospitalized after fighting Vegeta.

Kiwi

Master of evil! His hobby is to conquer and collect planets. Like Vegeta, Freeza wants to achieve eternal life. He seems to be much stronger than Vegeta.

Freeza's underling. Lives to defeat his rival Vegeta.

DRAGON BALL

YO!!! DID YOU MISS ME?

DBZ:56 • Goku Returns! Again!

Akira Toriyama
鳥山明 BIRD STUDIO

DRAGON BALL

EVERYONE'S WAITING!!
NOW IT'S TIME TO GO!!!

Akira Toriyama
鳥山明
BIRD STUDIO

DBZ :57 • Son Goku's Spaceship

DRAGON BALL

I'LL BECOME STRONGER STILL!

ドラゴンボール

Akira Toriyama
鳥山明
BIRD STUDIO

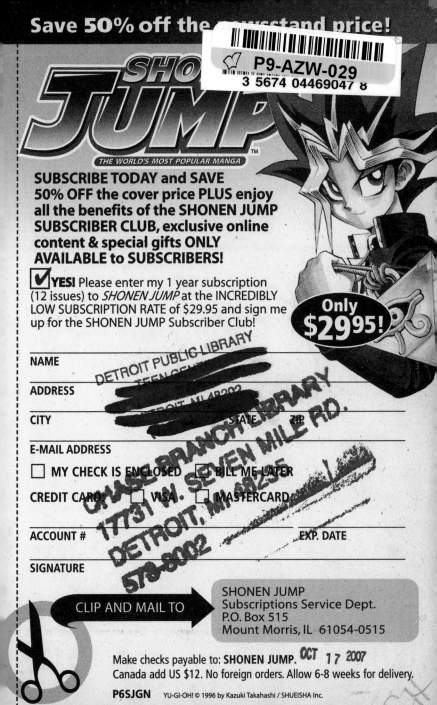